IMPROVING NUMERACY THROUGH SPREADSHEETS

Bob Sykes

Brilliant Publications

We hope you and your class enjoy using this book. Other books published by Brilliant Publications include:

Maths titles

How to be Brilliant at Mental Arithmetic	1 897675 21 6
How to be Brilliant at Algebra	1 897675 05 4
How to be Brilliant at Numbers	1 897675 06 2
How to be Brilliant at Shape and Space	1 897675 07 0
How to be Brilliant at Using a Calculator	1 897675 04 6

English titles

How to be Brilliant at Writing Stories	1 897675 00 3
How to be Brilliant at Writing Poetry	1 897675 01 1
How to be Brilliant at Grammar	1 897675 02 X
How to be Brilliant at Making Books	1 897675 03 8
How to be Brilliant at Reading	1 897675 09 7
How to be Brilliant at Spelling	1 897675 08 9

Science titles

How to be Brilliant at Science Investigations	1 897675 11 9
How to be Brilliant at Recording in Science	1 897675 10 0
How to be Brilliant at Materials	1 897675 12 7
How to be Brilliant at Electricity, Light and Sound	1 897675 13 5

If you would like further information on these or other titles published by Brilliant Publications, please write to the address given below.

Published by Brilliant Publications, The Old School Yard, Leighton Road, Northall, Dunstable, Bedfordshire LU6 2HA

Written by Bob Sykes
Illustrated by Virginia Gray

Printed in Malta by Interprint Ltd

© Bob Sykes 1999
ISBN 1 897675 53 4

First published 1999
10 9 8 7 6 5 4 3 2 1

The right of Bob Sykes to be identified as author of this work has been asserted by him in accordance with the Copyright, Designs and Patents Act 1988.

Pages 7, 9, 11, 13, 15, 17, 19, 21, 23, 25, 27, 29, 31, 33, 35, 37, 39, 41, 43, 45 and 47 may be photocopied by individual teachers for class use, without permission from the publisher. The material may not be produced in any other form or for any other purpose without the prior permission of the publisher.

Contents

	page
Links to the National Curriculum and the National Numeracy Project	4
General introduction to setting up spreadsheets	5
Yoghurts	6
Limousines	8
Sum difference	10
Addition pyramids	12
Dinosaur factory	14
Times table	16
Magic squares, 1	18
Adam and Eve sequences	20
Doughnuts	22
6-digit deltas	24
Puzzles	26
Area and perimeter	28
Temperature	30
Number patterns	32
Average scores	34
Number guesser—a game for two	36
Factors	38
Magic squares, 2	40
Exam results	42
Remaindermind	44
Throwing six dice	46
Starting points for further activities	48

Links to the National Curriculum and the National Numeracy Project

The National Curriculum
The Key Stage 2 programme of study states that pupils should be given the opportunity to use information technology to 'explore and solve problems in the context of work across a variety of subjects'. Pupils will be unable to use spreadsheets as a tool until they know exactly what spreadsheets can do. These worksheets are designed to teach pupils some of the basic skills of using spreadsheets. Many of the exercises have specific 'right answers' to motivate pupils and to increase their confidence. At the same time, extension activities are suggested which, when used appropriately by the teacher, can enable pupils to embark upon more open-ended investigations using the skills they have acquired.

Level descriptions – a selection of appropriate statements
At each level, pupils are able to use IT-based models or simulations to:

Level 2 – investigate options as they explore aspects of real and imaginary situations.

Level 3 – help them make decisions, and are aware of the consequences of their choices.

Level 4 – explore patterns and relationships, and make simple predictions about the consequences of their decision making.

The pupils are able to:

Level 5 – explore the effects of changing the variables in computer models.

The National Numeracy Project
The three main strands of the National Numeracy Project framework of objectives are as follows:
1.   knowledge of numbers and the number system;
2.   calculations;
3.   making sense of numerical problems.

Spreadsheets provide the perfect number environment in which pupils can practise and extend their understanding in these areas. All the activities in this book encourage pupils to use existing knowledge of number in new situations and encourage a confident use of number skills. Many of the ideas presented in these pages can be used as a basis for the oral mental session at the beginning of a mathematics lesson.

Using the worksheets
The pupil worksheets are on the right-hand pages. The facing left-hand pages give answers and advice for teachers.The worksheets can be used in a variety of ways. They can be used to enhance or introduce topic-based work in mathematics, as a springboard to open-ended IT investigation work or simply as a confidence-boosting exercise for pupils keen to learn about the workings of their computer. Having acquired skills and know-how, pupils should then develop the confidence to apply their knowledge to enhance their own studies in whatever area of the curriculum they are working.

General introduction to setting up spreadsheets

Look at this spreadsheet from the Yoghurts worksheet on page 7:

	A	B	C	D
1		How many?	Cost for one	Cost
2	Vanilla	2	29	58
3	Chocolate	2	24	48
4	Strawberry	2	33	66
5	Toffee	2	35	70
6	TOTAL	8		242

Each cell has a unique reference: A2, B5, etc. In this example cell A2 has the contents:

> Vanilla

To help pupils to understand the instructions on the worksheets, the following format has been used:

Bold script cells

Darker, bold script indicates contents which are entered exactly as shown on the sheet. So, in the Yoghurts worksheet, move to cell A2 and type in 'Vanilla'.

Calculation cells

Type which is not in bold shows cell contents that are the result of a calculation involving the contents of other cells. In the example above, D2 shows the number 58. However, the contents of cell D2 is the formula or equation:

> =B2*C2

This means that the number we see on the screen (58) in cell D2 is the product of the numbers entered in cells B2 and C2. If the number in cell B2 is altered, then the numbers in cell D2 (and cells B6 and D6) will also change.

Equations or formulae begin with the = sign.

Copied cells

Cells can be copied. This may involve highlighting and filling cells, or a more simple operation using the mouse, depending on the spreadsheet package you are using.

> **It is strongly recommended that teachers should work each exercise for themselves before working with pupils.**

Yoghurts

Information
Throughout this exercise, pence have been used, without the use of pounds.

It is important that pupils understand that some numbers which appear on screen do so as a result of a formula. It is also important that pupils understand that the * symbol means multiplication. Formulae start with the = symbol.

Answers
1. How much would it cost for 2 Vanilla, 2 Chocolate, 2 Strawberry and 2 Toffee yoghurts?   **242p**
2. How much would it cost for 3 Vanilla, 2 Chocolate, 2 Strawberry and 1 Toffee yoghurt? **236p**
3. What is the least that David can spend?   **217p**
4. What is the most that David can spend?   **261p**
5. If he spends 240p how many yoghurts of each flavour did he buy?
   2 Vanilla   2 Chocolate   3 Strawberry   1 Toffee
6. Work out how he can spend 222p.
   2 Vanilla   4 Chocolate   1 Strawberry   1 Toffee
7. Work out how he can spend 259p.
   1 Vanilla   1 Chocolate   2 Strawberry   4 Toffee

Extension activities
* When pupils make up their own problem, they can work with the existing worksheet or they can alter individual prices, or even the commodities on sale.

* The Limousines worksheet (page 9) is an extension of Yoghurts.

Yoghurts

David is sent to the shop to buy eight yoghurts. He has to buy at least one of each of these four flavours. How much does he spend?

Setting up the spreadsheet

Copy the **bold** words and numbers exactly as shown on the spreadsheet below. The other cells have contents as follows:

D2 | =B2*C2

D3 | =B3*C3

D4 | =B4*C4

D5 | =B5*C5

D6 | =D2+D3+D4+D5

B6 | =B2+B3+B4+B5

	A	B	C	D
1		How many?	Cost for one	Cost
2	Vanilla	2	29	58
3	Chocolate	2	24	48
4	Strawberry	2	33	66
5	Toffee	2	35	70
6	TOTAL	8		242

Change the numbers in column B, keeping the **total number of yoghurts as 8** and making sure David buys **at least one of each flavour.**

Answer these questions:

1. How much would it cost for 2 Vanilla, 2 Chocolate, 2 Strawberry and 2 Toffee yoghurts? _____

2. How much would it cost for 3 Vanilla, 2 Chocolate, 2 Strawberry and 1 Toffee yoghurt? _____

3. What is the least that David can spend? _____

4. What is the most that David can spend? _____

5. If he spends 240p how many yoghurts of each flavour did he buy?

   _____

6. Work out how he can spend 222p.

   _____

7. Work out how he can spend 259p.

   _____

Make up a problem like this one for a friend to solve.

Limousines

This is a direct extension of the Yoghurts worksheet (page 7).
Numbers involved are larger, involving thousands of pounds, and pence.
The use of the decimal point may need to be explained.

Answers

How much would it cost for two of each type of car?   **£ 205 270.42**

How much would it cost for 3 soft-tops, 2 estate cars and 2 limousines? **£161 955.88**

These are the instructions the father gives his son. What does he buy in each case?

1.   Here's two hundred thousand pounds. Bring me as little change as you can.

3 soft-tops	**1** limousines	**2** sports	**2** estates
Total cost	**£197 190.10**		

2.   Buy me six new cars, but spend between £150 000 and £155 000.

2 soft-tops	**2** limousines	**1** sports	**1** estates
Total cost	**£153 468.65**		

3.   Spend as near as you can to £122,000.

1 soft-tops	**1** limousines	**1** sports	**2** estates
Total cost	**£122 091.43**		

4.   Spend exactly £203 350.08.

1 soft-tops	**2** limousines	**2** sports	**3** estates
Total cost	£203 350.08		

Extension activities

*   Pupils can make up their own problems for each other using the above data. Pupils may also enter real data of their own—real cars, bikes or any other consumer products.

Limousines

A rich man has an enormous garage so he sends his son to buy some cars to fill up the empty space.

These are the cars he could buy. The garage only has **three** of each type.

	£21 376.56		£19 456.22	
Soft-top				Estate

	£32 345.55		£29 456.88	
Sports				Limousine

Setting up the spreadsheet

Set up a spreadsheet like you did in the Yoghurts worksheet, with the four cars and their prices, in columns. Then answer these questions.

How much would it cost for two of each type of car? £_____

How much would it cost for 3 soft-tops, 2 estate cars and 2 limousines? £_____

These are the instructions the father gives his son. What does he buy in each case?

1. Here's two hundred thousand pounds. Bring me as little change as you can.

    ___ soft-tops   ___ limousines   ___ sports   ___ estates

    Total cost _____

2. Buy me six new cars, but spend between £150 000 and £155 000.

    ___ soft-tops   ___ limousines   ___ sports   ___ estates

    Total cost _____

3. Spend as near as you can to £122 000.

    ___ soft-tops   ___ limousines   ___ sports   ___ estates

    Total cost _____

4. Spend exactly £203 350.08.

    ___ soft-tops   ___ limousines   ___ sports   ___ estates

    Total cost   £203 350.08

© Bob Sykes
This page may be photocopied.

Sum difference

Introduction
Pupils need to understand the terms 'sum' and 'difference'.

As an introductory activity, pupils can work some examples on paper. Start with problems such as, 'I have two numbers 3 and 7. What is the sum and what is the difference of these two numbers.' Then the pupils can be presented with problems where the sum and difference are given and pupils have to find the number. At this stage they may develop a strategy for finding an answer, but this is a discussion that can also take place after the spreadsheet activity.

Answers

First number	Second number	Sum	Difference
7	2	9	5
8	4	12	4
6	2	8	4
14	6	20	8
18	8	26	10
22	4	26	18
24	7	31	17
55	12	67	43
76	55	131	21
61	39	100	22

If the sum of two numbers is 24 and the difference is 10, what are the numbers? **17, 7**
If the sum of two numbers is 34 and the difference is 4, what are the numbers? **19, 15**

Extension activities
- Ask pupils to discuss and then write down their strategies for solving these problems. They can then present problems to each other to check their strategies.

- A whole new set of problems can be generated by changing column D to a product column, rather than difference. The problems then become, eg 'If the sum of two numbers is 9 and their product is 20, what are the numbers?'

Sum difference

Setting up the spreadsheet

A1 | First   B1 | Second   C1 | Sum   D1 | Difference

A2 | 7   B2 | 2   C2 | =A2+B2   D2 | =ABS(A2–B2)

	A	B	C	D
1	First	Second	Sum	Difference
2	7	2	9	5
3				
4				

Try different numbers in A2 and B2 and solve these problems.
It doesn't matter about the order of the two numbers. Complete this table.

First number	Second number	Sum	Difference
7	2	9	5
		12	4
		8	4
		20	8
		26	10
		26	18
		31	17
		67	43
		131	21
		100	22

If the sum of two numbers is 24 and the difference is 10, what are the numbers? _____

If the sum of two numbers is 34 and the difference is 4, what are the numbers? _____

© Bob Sykes
This page may be photocopied.

Addition pyramids

Introduction
Work some examples with pupils on paper. Make sure pupils understand the concept of re-arranging the numbers, ie using the number once only.

Answers
These answers are not unique.

3	1	2	4	→	16
4	1	3	2	→	18
4	2	3	1	→	20
1	4	2	3	→	22
1	3	4	2	→	24

What is the highest total you could achieve with these digits?

2	5	5	2	→	**34**

What is the lowest total you could achieve with these digits?

7	1	3	5	→	**24**

Extension activities
- Ask pupils to explain high and low totals and discuss strategies.

- Use the numbers –1, 1, –2, 2 to make a total 0.

- Algebraic approach: if the four digits are represented by a, b, c, d then the total is represented by $a + 3b + 3c + d$

- Extend the number of digits to six. Discuss strategies for maximizing the total.

- Multiply, instead of adding numbers to generate the number above in the pyramid. Using the digits 1, 2, 3, 4, what are the maximum and minimum totals? (Answers: 96 and 3,456.)

Addition pyramids

In an addition pyramid, each number is the total of the two below it.

Setting up the spreadsheet

A4 [4]	B3 [=A4+C4]	C2 [=B3+D3]	C4 [2]
D1 [=C2+E2]	D3 [=C4+E4]	E2 [=D3+F3]	E4 [3]
F3 [=E4+G4]	G4 [1]		

	A	B	C	D	E	F	G	H
1				20				
2			11		9			
3		6		5		4		
4	4		2		3		1	
5								

The pyramid total is shown in D1.

Re-arrange the four numbers in A4, C4, E4 and G4 to make different totals. Only five different totals are possible. Show how it is possible to get each of these totals.

_____	_____	_____	_____	→	16
_____	_____	_____	_____	→	18
4	2	3	1	→	20
_____	_____	_____	_____	→	22
_____	_____	_____	_____	→	24

What is the highest total you could achieve with these digits?

2	2	5	5	→	_____

What is the lowest total you could achieve with these digits?

1	3	5	7	→	_____

© Bob Sykes
This page may be photocopied.

Dinosaur factory

Introduction
Pupils should know that:
- The = sign comes before a formula.
- The * sign is the multiplcation symbol.

Answers

How much would it cost for 12 dinosaurs?   **£29.04**

How much would it cost for 36 dinosaurs?   **£87.12**

How much would it cost for the poppers for 19 dinosaurs?   **£6.65**

How much would it cost for the legs for 5 dinosaurs?   **£2.10**

How many poppers are needed for 7 dinosaurs?   **35**

Alter the number in cell B1 and numbers in column C to answer these.

If legs cost 27p how much would 1 dinosaur cost?   **£2.54**

If legs cost 27p how much would 12 dinosaurs cost?   **£30.48**

If legs are 27p and poppers cost 8p each, how much would it cost for

20 dinosaurs? **£51.80**

Extension activities
- **Beetles!**
  Plastic beetles are made of 1 body, 1 head, 2 feelers, 1 tail, 2 eyes and 6 legs. Pupils can make up prices and problems like the ones above for other pupils to solve.

Dinosaur factory

In the factory, toy dinosaurs are made up of one body, one head, two arms and two legs. These parts are held together with five poppers. Set up a spreadsheet to calculate the cost of making the dinosaurs.

Setting up the spreadsheet

Copy down the **bold** words and figures directly from the spreadsheet. The numbers which are not in bold print are formulas:

B2 `=B1`   B3 `=B2`   B4 `=B1*2`

B5 `=B1*2`   B6 `=B1*5`   D2 `=B2*C2`

D3 `=B3*C3`   D4 `=B4*C4`   D5 `=B5*C5`

D6 `=B6*C6`   D7 `=D2+D3+D4+D5+D6`

	A	B	C	D
1	No. of Dinosaurs	1	Price each (p)	Price
2	Heads	1	34	34
3	Body	1	67	67
4	Arms	2	32	64
5	Legs	2	21	42
6	Poppers	5	7	35
7			Total cost	242

Now alter the number in cell B1 to answer the following questions.

How much would it cost for 12 dinosaurs?_____

How much would it cost for 36 dinosaurs? _____

How much would it cost for the poppers for 19 dinosaurs?_____

How much would it cost for the legs for 5 dinosaurs? _____

How many poppers are needed for 7 dinosaurs? _____

Alter the number in cell B1 and numbers in column C to answer these questions.

If legs cost 27p how much would 1 dinosaur cost? _____

If legs cost 27p how much would 12 dinosaurs cost? _____

If legs are 27p and poppers cost 8p each, how much would it cost for

20 dinosaurs? _____

© Bob Sykes
This page may be photocopied.

Times table

Answers

Last digits

2 times table	2	4	6	8	0	2	4	6	8	0
3 times table	3	6	9	2	5	8	1	4	7	0
4 times table	4	8	2	6	0	4	8	2	6	0
5 times table	5	0	5	0	5	0	5	0	5	0
6 times table	6	2	8	4	0	6	2	8	4	0
7 times table	7	4	1	8	5	2	9	6	3	0
8 times table	8	6	4	2	0	8	6	4	2	0
9 times table	9	8	7	6	5	4	3	2	1	0
10 times table	0	0	0	0	0	0	0	0	0	0

Extension activities

• Continue the spreadsheet to investigate patterns up to the 20 times table.

• Type in different numbers in A1 to generate an even greater variety of times tables.

• **Square numbers**
Change cell C1 to **=A1** and then copy and fill C1 down to C10. Ask pupils to copy down the list of square numbers.

Times table

Setting up the spreadsheet

A1 | `1`

B1 | `times`

C1 | `7`

D1 | `is`

E1 | `=A1*C1`

A2 | `=A1+1`

C2 | `C1+0`

Now copy A2 and fill all the cells down to A10.
copy B1 and fill all the cells down to B10.
copy C2 and fill all the cells down to C10.
copy D1 and fill all the cells down to D10.
copy E1 and fill all the cells down to E10.

	A	B	C	D	E
1	**1**	times	**7**	is	**7**
2	2	times	7	is	14
3	3	times	7	is	21
4	4	times	7	is	28
5	5	times	7	is	35

Type in different numbers in cell C1 and generate different times tables.

Last digits

Look at the last digit of the numbers in these times tables and write down the pattern that you see.

2 times table _____

3 times table _____

4 times table _____

5 times table _____

6 times table _____

7 times table   7   4   1   8   5   2   9   6   3   0

8 times table _____

9 times table _____

10 times table _____

© Bob Sykes
This page may be photocopied.

Magic squares, 1

Answer

There are many possible answers. Here are two:

4	3	8
9	5	1
2	7	6

2	9	4
7	5	3
6	1	8

Extension activities

- **Three different sets of numbers**
  Use the digits 2, 5, 7, 8, 12, 13, 15, 18 to make all totals 30.
  Use the digits 12, 13, 14, 15, 16, 17, 18, 19, 20 to make all totals the same.
  Use the digits 1, 7, 13, 31, 37, 43, 61, 67, 73 to make all totals the same.

- **Magic square game**
  Player 1 can use the odd numbers 1, 3, 5, 7, 9 once only.
  Player 2 can use the even numbers 2, 4, 6, 8 once only.
  Player 1 starts by playing any one of his numbers anywhere on the magic square.
  Player 2 continues by playing one of her numbers.
  The winner is the first player to make the total of any row or column to be 15.

- **Antimagic square**
  Use the digits 1 to 9 once only. Make all the rows, columns and diagonals add to different totals.

- **Negative number square**
  Use the numbers –4, –3, –2, –1, 0, 1, 2, 3, 4 to make all totals 0.

- **Multiplying magic squares**
  Instead of adding cells, alter the spreadsheet to multiply cells to make the totals.
  Use the numbers 1, 2, 3, 4, 6, 9, 12, 18, 36 to make all totals 216.
  Use the numbers 1, 3, 4, 9, 12, 16, 36, 48, 144 to make all totals the same.

Magic squares, 1

In a magic square all the horizontal, vertical and diagonal rows add up to the same number.

Setting up the spreadsheet

Copy the **bold** numbers exactly as shown on the spreadsheet below. The other cells have contents as follows:

E2   `=B2+C2+D2`   E3   `=B3+C3+D3`

E4   `=B4+C4+D4`   E5   `=B2+C3+D4`

A5   `=B4+C3+D2`   B5   `=B2+B3+B4`

C5   `=C2+C3+C4`   D5   `=D2+D3+D4`

If you know how, you should put a thick border around the magic square.

	A	B	C	D	E
1					
2		**1**	**2**	**3**	6
3		**4**	**5**	**6**	15
4		**7**	**8**	**9**	24
5	15	12	15	18	15
6					

The magic square challenge

Using the numbers 1 to 9 once only, put them in the magic square so that all the horizontal, vertical and diagonal columns add up to the same number.

© Bob Sykes
This page may be photocopied.

Adam and Eve sequences

Answers

(1, 2)	→	**34**	(2, 1)	→	**29**	(0, 0)	→	**0**
(3, 1)	→	**37**	(2, 3)	→	**55**	(8, 8)	→	**168**
(1, 0)	→	**8**	(2, 0)	→	**16**	(0, 5)	→	**65**
(1, 4)	→	60	(1, 7)	→	99	(2, 8)	→	120
(6, 4)	→	100	(7, 7)	→	147	(2, 4)	→	68

Extension activities

- Instead of adding two cells to find the next, change the equation in cell C1 (and copy it to the right) so that the third cell is the positive difference between the two previous cells.

C1 | =ABS(A1–B1)

- Pupils can then investigate the number patterns that are generated.
- What if the first number is 0?
- What if the second number is 0?
- What if the first and second numbers are the same?
- What if the second number is 1?
- Now complete this table by filling in the eighth number in the sequence each time.

1st→ 2nd ↓	0	1	2	3	4	5
0						
1						
2						
3						
4						
5						

Answers

1st→ 2nd ↓	0	1	2	3	4	5
0	0	0	0	0	0	0
1	1	1	1	1	1	1
2	2	0	2	0	2	0
3	3	1	1	3	1	1
4	4	0	0	0	4	0
5	5	1	1	1	1	5

Adam and Eve sequences

An Adam and Eve sequence starts with two numbers, Adam and Eve.
Add up the two previous numbers to find the next.
The proper word for an Adam and Eve sequence is a Fibonacci sequence.

Setting up the spreadsheet

A1 `1`   B1 `1`   C1 `=A1+B1`

Then copy C1 and fill all the cells to H1

	A	B	C	D	E	F	G	H
1	**1**	**1**	2	3	5	8	13	21
2								
3								
4								
5								

Now alter the numbers in A1 and B1 and note the number in column H, which is the 8th number in the sequence.

(Adam, Eve)	→	8th number
(1,1)	→	21

Now find out the eighth number in these Adam and Eve questions.

(1, 2) → ____   (2, 1) → ____   (0, 0) → ____

(3, 1) → ____   (2, 3) → ____   (8, 8) → ____

(1, 0) → ____   (2, 0) → ____   (0, 5) → ____

Now, by experimenting with different pairs of Adam and Eve numbers, try to get the following eighth number. (Adam and Eve are both less then 9.)

(__, __) →   60   (__, __) →   99   (__, __) →   120

(__, __) →   100   (__, __) →   147   (__, __) →   68

© Bob Sykes
This page may be photocopied.

Doughnuts

Answers

Place the numbers 1, 2, 3, 4, 5, 6, 7 and 8 once only in the doughnut, so that the four rows and columns totals are 12. Write your answer below.

2	7	3
4		8
6	5	1

This time make all totals 13. Write your answer below.

8	3	2
4		6
1	7	5

This time make all totals 14. Write your answer below.

5	6	3
1		7
8	2	4

Extension activity

- Using the numbers 19, 10, 31, 22, 13, 34, 25 and 16 place them on the doughnut to make all four totals 69.

Answer

16	19	34
22		10
31	13	25

Doughnuts

The numbers 1 to 8 are arranged as shown on the spreadsheet.
These numbers are in a doughnut shape around cell B2 which is left blank.
The other four filled cells contain the sum of rows and columns.

Setting up the spreadsheet

A1 [1]   B1 [2]   C1 [3]   A2 [8]

C2 [4]   A3 [7]   B3 [6]   C3 [5]

D1 [=A1+B1+C1]   D3 [=A3+B3+C3]

A4 [=A1+A2+A3]   C4 [=C1+C2+C3]

	A	B	C	D
1	1	2	3	6
2	8		4	
3	7	6	5	18
4	16		12	
5				

If you know how, shade in cell B2, the centre of the doughnut, and put a thick border around the doughnut.

Place the numbers 1, 2, 3, 4, 5, 6, 7 and 8 once only in the doughnut, so that the four rows and columns totals are 12. Write your answer below.

This time make all totals 13. Write your answer below.

This time make all totals 14. Write your answer below.

© Bob Sykes
This page may be photocopied.

6-digit deltas

Information

Arrange the six digits 0 to 5 in any order, put them together in pairs to make three two-digit numbers and then process the difference between these numbers as follows to make a final total, which is 5 in this example. Pupils might like to try this with a calculator as an introductory exercise, trying to get as large a total as possible. You may need to do some work on how the digits can be re-arranged.

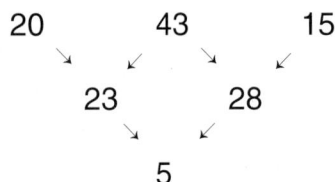

$$20 \qquad 43 \qquad 15$$

$$23 \qquad 28$$

$$5$$

The example above has a final total of 5. With six digits, the smallest possible total is 0, the largest is 42. Pupils need to be reminded that they must use each of the digits 0 to 5 once only.

Spreadsheet

This activity uses the ABS command, which calculates the absolute value of a calculation, ignoring negatives. So ABS(8–4) would be 4 and ABS(4–8) would also be 4.

The work on the second part of the worksheet is quite difficult.

Answers

(12,54,03)→9   (50,12,34)→16   (45,10,32)→31

There are only four arrangements of numbers which will give final numbers as follows.

(10,42,35)→25	(35,42,10)→25	(20,13,45)→25	(45,13,20)→25
(05,42,31)→26	(31,42,05)→26	(24,13,50)→26	(50,13,24)→26
(01,42,35)→34	(35,42,01)→34	(20,13,54)→34	(54,13,20)→34
(03,52,41)→38	(41,52,03)→38	(14,03,52)→38	(52,03,14)→38
(01,52,43)→42	(43,52,01)→42	(12,03,54)→42	(54,03,12)→42

Extension activities

- Not all the numbers between 0 and 42 are possible. Which numbers less than 20 are possible? Which numbers more than 30?
  Answer: These numbers are **not** possible to find: 1, 2, 4, 10, 20, 35, 36, 37, 40.

- Using the digits 0 to 9 once each to make five two-digit numbers, arrange them in a digit delta as above and try to make the highest final number as possible. (78 is the highest total found so far.)
  Answer: (27, 15, 04, 96, 83)→78
  (This is a very difficult activity, due to the large number of different arrangements possible, though it is possible to invent some strategies for maximizing the final total.)

6-digit deltas

Setting up the spreadsheet

A1 | 20   C1 | 43   E1 | 15

B2 | ABS(A1–C1)   D2 | ABS(C1–E1)   C3 | ABS(B2–D2)

	A	B	C	D	E	F
1	20		43		15	
2		23		28		
3			5			
4						

Arrange the six digits 0 to 5 in any order and put them together in pairs to make three two-digit nunbers. Put these in A1, C1 and E1 and then see the result displayed in C3. **Use each of the 6 digits once only.**

What do these arrangements of numbers have as their result?

A1 12   C1 54   E1 03   → ____

A1 50   C1 12   E1 34   → ____

A1 45   C1 10   E1 32   → ____

Try to find an arrangement of the six digits which will give you results as below. (42 is the largest possible number.)

A1 ____   C1 ____   E1 ____   → 25

A1 ____   C1 ____   E1 ____   → 26

A1 ____   C1 ____   E1 ____   → 34

A1 ____   C1 ____   E1 ____   → 38

A1 ____   C1 ____   E1 ____   → 42

© Bob Sykes
This page may be photocopied.

Puzzles

Simple exercises can be worked with pupils on paper. In algebraic terms, the mathematical exercise that is being carried out is (a + b) x c. You may need to explain that the brackets mean that the numbers inside the brackets must be added first.

Work on the spreadsheet need not use more than one row, with different numbers being placed in cells A1 and C1.

Answers

Use 2 3 4	2	plus	4	times	3	equals	18
Use 5 6 7	5	plus	6	times	7	equals	77
Use 7 9 10	9	plus	7	times	10	equals	160
Use 2 9 12	12	plus	9	times	2	equals	42
Use 3 12 15	15	plus	12	times	3	equals	81
Use 8 9 14	14	plus	8	times	9	equals	198
Use 12 13 19	12	plus	19	times	13	equals	403
Use 14 18 20	14	plus	18	times	20	equals	640
Use 18 24 36	24	plus	36	times	18	equals	1080
Use 19 23 17	17	plus	23	times	19	equals	760

Extension activities

*   Ask pupils to make up their own problems.

*   Given three numbers, how many different totals are possible?

*   If you use three consecutive numbers in order, what are the numbers needed to give these totals?

77	(5, 6, 7)	20	(2, 3, 4)	104	(6, 7, 8)
350	(12, 13, 14)	170	(8, 9, 10)		

Puzzles

Set up a spreadsheet to help you solve some number puzzles. In these puzzles, the numbers in A1 and C1 are added before they are multiplied by the number in E1.

Setting up the spreadsheet

A1 | 2   B1 | plus   C1 | 4

D1 | times   E1 | 3   F1 | equals

G1 | =(A1+C1)*E1

	A	B	C	D	E	F	G
1	2	plus	4	times	3	equals	18
2							
3							
4							

Now use the spreadsheet to help you solve these puzzles.

Use 2 3 4		plus		times		equals	18
Use 5 6 7		plus		times		equals	77
Use 7 9 10		plus		times		equals	160
Use 2 9 12		plus		times		equals	42
Use 3 12 15		plus		times		equals	81
Use 8 9 14		plus		times		equals	198
Use 12 13 19		plus		times		equals	403
Use 14 18 20		plus		times		equals	640
Use 18 24 36		plus		times		equals	1080
Use 19 23 17		plus		times		equals	760

© Bob Sykes
This page may be photocopied.

Area and perimeter

Answers

Length	0	1	2	3	4	5	6	7	8	9	10	11	12
Breadth	12	11	10	9	8	7	6	5	4	3	2	1	0
Area	0	11	20	27	32	35	36	35	32	27	20	11	0

What value of length gives the greatest area? **6 cm**

What shape is this?   **Square**

Describe the shape that has length 12 cm and breadth 0 cm.   **A flat line (or similar)**

Extension activities

*   Pupils can draw these rectangles on paper.

*   Pupils can graph results with length on the horizontal axis and area on the vertical axis.

Area and perimeter

Investigation

If the perimeter of a rectangle is 24 cm, what is the area?
If the perimeter is 24 cm then the length and breadth must add up to 12 cm.
Perimeter = Length + Length + Breadth + Breadth
Area = Length * Breadth

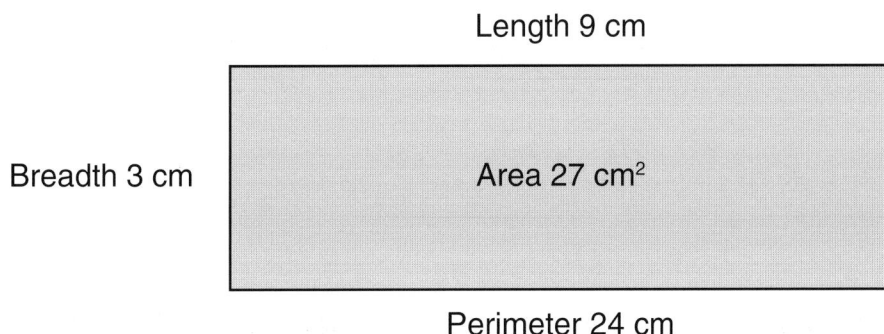

Length 9 cm

Breadth 3 cm

Area 27 cm^2

Perimeter 24 cm

Setting up the spreadsheet

A1	Length	B1	Breadth	C1	Perimeter
D1	Area	A2	9	B2	=12–A2
C2	=A2+A2+B2+B2	D2	=A2*B2		

	A	B	C	D
1	Length	Breadth	Perimeter	Area
2	9	3	24	27
3				
4				

Try different lengths by typing in the numbers 0 to 12 in cell A2.
Each time record the breadth and area in the table below.

Length	0	1	2	3	4	5	6	7	8	9	10	11	12
Breadth										3			
Area										27			

What value of length gives the greatest area? _____

What shape is this?_____

Describe the shape that has length 12 cm and breadth 0 cm. _____

Temperature

Introduction

Pupils may have a working knowledge of temperature and may be able to discuss the use of Celsius and Fahrenheit scales with reference to weather, body temperature and cooking.

Pupils may need some discussion of negative numbers. Parallel Celsius and Fahrenheit scales drawn on card may help.

Answers

100°C	=	**32°F**	30°C	=	**86°F**	10°C	=	**50°F**
19°C	=	**66.2°F**	0°C	=	**32°F**	−10°C	=	**14°F**
35°C	=	**95°F**	**70°C**	=	158°F	**−15°C**	=	5°F
20°C	=	**68°F**	**0°C**	=	**32°F**	**−5°C**	=	23°F

Extension activities

• Pupils can graph their results on graph paper.

Temperature

Converting Celsius to Fahrenheit

It is common to measure temperature in two ways. One is the Fahrenheit scale (°F) and the other is the Celsius scale (°C).

Water freezes at 0°C which is 32°F.   0° C = 32°F

Water boils at 100°C which is 212°F.   100 °C = 212°F

Set up a spreadsheet which will make it easy for you to convert from one temperature scale to another.

Setting up the spreadsheet

A1 | Celsius   B1 | Fahrenheit

A2 | 100   B2 | =32+(A2*9)/5

	A	B	C	D
1	Celsius	Fahrenheit		
2	100	212		
3				
4				
5				
6				

Now change the number in A2 and read the answers in B2.

100°F   =   _____ °F   30°C   =   _____ °F   10°C   =   _____ °F

19°C   =   _____ °F   0°C   =   _____ °F   −10°C   =   _____ °F

Now try different numbers in cell A2 till you find the correct number in B2.

_____ °C = 95°F   _____ °C = 158°F   _____ °C = 5°F

_____ °C = 68°F   _____ °C = 32°F   _____ °C = 23°F

Number patterns

Answers

Start with 2 and add on 3.

| 2 | **5** | **8** | **11** | **14** | **17** | **20** | **23** |

Start with 23 and add on 3.

| 23 | **26** | **29** | **32** | **35** | **38** | **41** | **44** |

Start with 30 and subtract 3.

| 30 | **27** | **24** | **21** | **18** | **15** | **12** | **9** |

Start with 0 and add on 25.

| 0 | **25** | **50** | **75** | **100** | **125** | **150** | **175** |

Start with 876 and add on 876.

| 876 | **1 752** | **2 628** | **3 504** | **4 380** | **5 256** | **6 132** | **7 008** |

Add on 9 each time, 8th term = 80.

| **17** | **26** | **35** | **44** | 53 | 62 | 71 | 80 |

Add on 13 each time, 8th term = 108.

| **17** | **30** | **43** | **56** | 69 | 82 | 95 | 108 |

Add on 55 each time, 8th term 440.

| **55** | **110** | **165** | **220** | 275 | 330 | 385 | 440 |

Subtract 5 each time, 8th term = 48.

| **83** | **78** | **73** | **68** | 63 | 58 | 53 | 48 |

Subtract 9 each time, 8th term = 21.

| **84** | **75** | **66** | **57** | 48 | 39 | 30 | 21 |

Extension activities

- Pupils can be given problems which test their understanding of decimals, eg start with 3 and add on 0.4.

- Other problems can be created which introduce pupils to the idea of negative numbers, eg start with 5 and subtract 3.

Number patterns

Setting up the spreadsheet

A1 | 2 | B1 | =A1+3 |

Copy and fill B1 right to H1.

	A	B	C	D	E	F	G	H
1	**2**	5	8	11	14	17	20	23
2								
3								
4								
5								

Now set up these number patterns on the spreadsheet and copy the numbers on to the lines below. Clear all cells after each question.

Start with 2 and add on 3.

2 ___ ___ ___ ___ ___ ___ ___

Start with 23 and add on 3.

23 ___ ___ ___ ___ ___ ___ ___

Start with 30 and subtract 3.

30 ___ ___ ___ ___ ___ ___ ___

Start with 0 and add on 25.

0 ___ ___ ___ ___ ___ ___ ___

Start with 876 and add on 876.

876 ___ ___ ___ ___ ___ ___ ___

Add on 9 each time, 8th term = 80.

___ ___ ___ ___ ___ ___ ___ 80

Add on 13 each time, 8th term = 108.

___ ___ ___ ___ ___ ___ ___ 108

Add on 55 each time, 8th term = 440.

___ ___ ___ ___ ___ ___ ___ 440

Subtract 5 each time, 8th term = 48.

___ ___ ___ ___ ___ ___ ___ 48

Subtract 9 each time, 8th term = 21.

___ ___ ___ ___ ___ ___ ___ 21

© Bob Sykes
This page may be photocopied.

Average scores

Answers

Jane has an average score of 75.75, but gets a chance to retake test H.
What is her target for test H if she is to get an average score of 80%?
91%

Philip's scores for the same tests are as follows:

Test	A	B	C	D	E	F	G	H
Score	55	45	66	77	88	64	10	55

What is his average score for the eight tests?   **57.5**%
Philip gets a chance to retake test G. His retake score is 59. What is his new average
score for the eight tests?   **63.625**%

Monica's scores are as follows:

Test	A	B	C	D	E	F	G	H
Score	34	26	44	43	41	40	44	50

What is Monica's average score for the eight tests?   **40.25**%
If her retake score on test B is 12, what is her new average score?   **38.5**%

Extension activity

• Use real data from pupils' own scores on a new spreadsheet.

Average scores

Jane has to take 8 maths tests. Each test is out of 100. She sets herself a target to reach an average score for the 8 tests of at least 80 per cent.

Setting up the spreadsheet

Copy the spreadsheet on to the screen. Cell B10 is a formula.

B10 $\boxed{\text{=AVG(B2:B9)}}$ On some spreadsheets this needs to be written as:

     B10 $\boxed{\text{=AVERAGE(B2:B9)}}$

	A	B	C	D
1	Test	Score		
2	A	67		
3	B	72		
4	C	77		
5	D	67		
6	E	88		
7	F	88		
8	G	90		
9	H	57		
10	Average	75.75		

Jane has an average score of 75.75, but gets a chance to retake test H.
What is her target for test H if she is to get an average score of 80%?   _____%

Philip's scores for the same tests are as follows:

Test	A	B	C	D	E	F	G	H
Score	55	45	66	77	88	64	10	55

Copy these scores on to the spreadsheet in place of Jane's scores.
What is his average score for the eight tests?   _____%
Philip gets a chance to retake test G. His retake score is 59. What is his new average score for the eight tests?   _____%

Monica's scores are as follows:

Test	A	B	C	D	E	F	G	H
Score	34	26	44	43	41	40	44	50

What is Monica's average score for the eight tests?   _____%
If her retake score on test B is 12, what is her new average score?   _____%

Number guesser—a game for two

Introduction
In the example given on the worksheet, player 1 enters 43 into A1.
Player 2 takes ten guesses. Five guesses are too high and are copied automatically to column C.
Player 2 has a final guess of 43 which is correct.

At the end of the game, column B should be cleared.
Player 2 enters a new mystery number for player 1 to guess.

Rules
Pupils should decide the range of numbers allowed for each game.

eg   Whole numbers less than 100;
       Whole numbers less than 1000.

Players who need more than 18 guesses should give up.

Introductory activities
Play 'Number guesser' as a pencil/paper activity in pairs or as a class.
Discuss tactics on making guesses.

Extension activities
*   The range of numbers could include:
    eg numbers less than 10 correct to 1 decimal place;
         numbers less than 1 correct to 3 decimal places;
         whole numbers between −100 and +100.

*   What is the best tactic for making a guess?

*   Make up a table, which shows the minimum number of guesses needed for any mystery number in a given range.
    eg What is the minimum number of guesses that would guarantee finding any unknown whole number less than 64?

Number guesser—a game for two

Player 1 enters a mystery number in Cell A1.
Player 2 makes guesses in column B.
Guesses which are too high are automatically copied to column C.
Player 2 has to guess the number in the least possible number of guesses.
Players 1 and 2 swap roles for the next game.
In this example, suppose player 1 enters a mystery number 43 in A1.
You will need to use the " " symbols which are obtained by pressing shift 2.

Setting up the spreadsheet

A1 | 43 |

A2 | =A1 |

C1 | =IF(B1>A1,B1,"") |

D1 | =IF(A1=B1,"Correct","") |

Copy and fill A2 down to A18.
Copy and fill C1 down to C18.
Copy and fill D1 down to D18.

Now change the colour of the type in column A to white so it becomes invisible on screen.
If you can't do this, then use a piece of card and Blu-tack on the screen to hide column A.

	A	B	C	D	E
1	43	99	99		
2	43	10			
3	43	50	50		
4	43	40			
5	43	41			
6	43	46	46		
7	43	45	45		
8	43	42			
9	43	44	44		
10	43	43		Correct	
11	43				
12	43				
13	43				
14	43				
15	43				
16	43				
17	43				
18	43				

To start a new game, clear all the numbers from column B, then type a new mystery number in A1.

© Bob Sykes
This page may be photocopied.

Factors

Answers

Answer these questions for numbers up to 15.
Which numbers have 3 as a factor?   **3, 6, 9, 12, 15**
Which numbers have 5 as a factor?   **5, 10, 15**
Which numbers have 2 and 3 as factors? **6, 12**
Which number has 2 and 5 as a factor? **10**
Which number has 3 and 5 as a factor? **15**

Now fill and copy all the four cells A16, B16, C16 and D17 down to row 100.

Answer these questions for numbers up to 100.
Which numbers have 3 and 5 as factors?   **15, 30, 45, 60, 75, 90**
Which numbers have 2 and 5 as factors? **10, 20, 30, 40, 50, 60, 70, 80, 90, 100**
Which numbers have 2 3 and 5 as factors? **30, 60, 90**
Which numbers larger than 91 and less than 100 have 3 as a factor? **93, 96, 99**
Will 3 divide into 73? **NO**

Extensions

* Extra columns can be added, eg Fact 7, Fact 11.

* By inserting columns for Fact 1 and so on, then a thorough investigation of factors can lead to work on prime numbers, prime factors and square numbers.

    * A prime number has just two factors, eg the factors of 7 are 1 and 7.

    * The prime factors of 12 are 2 and 3.

    * Square numbers have an odd number of factors, eg 9 has three factors: 1, 3 and 9.

Factors

This spreadsheet tells you some of the factors of numbers up to 15.

Setting up the spreadsheet

A1	Number	B1	Fact 2	C1	Fact 3
D1	Fact 5	A2	1	B2	=MOD(A2,2)
C2	=MOD(A2,3)	D2	=MOD(A2,5)	A3	=A2+1

Copy and fill cell A3 down to A16. Copy and fill cell B2 down to B16
Copy and fill cell C2 down to C16. Copy and fill cell D2 down to D16
Only the first six rows are shown below.

	A	B	C	D
1	Number	Fact 2	Fact 3	Fact 5
2	**1**	1	1	1
3	2	0	2	2
4	3	1	0	3
5	4	0	1	4
6	5	1	2	0

The numbers in columns B, C and D are remainders. A remainder of 0 indicates a factor. So, for example, if the figure in column B is 0 then that indicates that 2 is a factor of the corresponding number in column A (2 and 4 in the spreadsheet above).

Answer these questions for numbers up to 15.

Which numbers have 3 as a factor? _____

Which numbers have 5 as a factor? _____

Which numbers have 2 and 3 as factors? _____

Which number has 2 and 5 as a factor? _____

Which number has 3 and 5 as a factor? _____

Now fill and copy all the four cells A16, B16, C16 and D17 down to row 100.

Answer these questions for numbers up to 100.

Which numbers have 3 and 5 as factors? _____

Which numbers have 2 and 5 as factors? _____

Which numbers have 2, 3 and 5 as factors? _____

Which numbers larger than 91 and less than 100 have 3 as a factor? _____

Will 3 divide into 73? _____

© Bob Sykes
This page may be photocopied.

Magic squares, 2

Answers

	A	B	C	D	E	F
1						
2		13	8	12	1	34
3		3	10	6	15	34
4		2	11	7	14	34
5		16	5	9	4	34
6	34	34	34	34	34	34

4	9	5	16
14	7	11	2
15	6	10	3
1	12	8	13

16	2	3	13
5	11	10	8
9	7	6	12
4	14	15	1

17	59	56	26
50	32	35	41
38	44	47	29
53	23	20	62

96	11	89	68
88	69	91	16
61	86	18	99
19	98	66	81

Extension activity

- Place the numbers 0, 1, 2, 3 and 4 five times each in a 5 x 5 magic square to make each row, column and diagonal add up to 10.

Answer to extension activity

0	1	2	3	4
3	4	0	1	2
1	2	3	4	0
4	0	1	2	3
2	3	4	0	1

Magic squares, 2

In a magic square all the horizontal, vertical and diagonal rows add up to the same number.

Setting up the spreadsheet

Copy the bold numbers exactly as shown on the spreadsheet below. The other cells have contents as shown below.

A6 `=B5+C4+D3+E2`   F6 `=B2+C3+D4+E5`

B6 `=B2+B3+B4+B5`   F2 `=B2+C2+D2+E2`

Copy and fill right B6 to E6. Copy and fill down F2 to F5.
If you know how, you should put a thick border around the magic square.

	A	B	C	D	E	F
1						
2			8	12		20
3			10	6	15	31
4			11			11
5		16	5		4	25
6	33	16	34	18	19	14

Put in the missing numbers 1, 2, 3, 7, 9, 13 and 14 in the square above to make each horizontal, vertical and diagonal row total the same.

Do the same with these two incomplete magic squares. Use the numbers 1 to 16 once each.

4			16
	7	11	
	6	10	3
	12		13

16			13
	11	10	8
		6	12
	4	14	

Put the numbers 17, 20, 41, 44, 53, 59 and 62 in the empty cells below to make each total 158.

		56	26
50	32	35	
38		47	29
	23		

Put in the numbers 61, 66, 68, 69, 88 and 96 in the empty cells below to make each total 264.

	11	89	
		91	16
	86	18	99
19	98		

© Bob Sykes
This page may be photocopied.

Exam results

Introduction
Pupils need to be familiar with the highlighting and sorting procedure before they attempt to sort their data. In this exercise it is important that pupils always highlight the rectangle from A2 to E9 before sorting.

Answers

1. What is the mean Maths score?   **60.125**

2. What is the mean English score?   **64.25**

3. What is the mean Science score?   **67**

4. What is the mean total score?   **191.375**

5. What is Bhavna's total score?   **178**

6. Who has the third highest Maths score?   **Dee**

7. Who is in the top three scores for all subjects?   **Dee**

8. How many pupils have above average Maths scores?   **3**

9. Who has the fifth highest Science score?   **Eve**

10. Who has the fourth highest total score?   **Adam**

11. How many pupils have a higher English score than Fee?   **4**

12. How many pupils have a higher Science score than Grant?   **5**

13. Who has the highest total score? **Dee**

14. Who has the lowest total score?   **Fee**

Extension activity
- Pupils can make up more questions using the above data, use their own invented data or use real pupil results.

Exam results

Eight pupils take three exams. Set up a spreadsheet to show their scores. Work out average scores for each test and the total scores.

Setting up the spreadsheet

Copy down the bold words and numbers directly on to the spreadsheet. Other cells contain formulae as follows:

B10 `=AVG(B2:B9)`   E2 `=B2+C2+D2`

On some spreadsheets B10 needs to be written as: B10 `=AVERAGE(B2:B9)`

Copy and fill E2 down to E9. Copy and fill B10 right to E10.

	A	B	C	D	E
1		Maths	English	Science	Total
2	Adam	78	65	55	198
3	Bhavna	56	55	67	
4	Chris	34	46	88	
5	Dee	66	75	93	
6	Eve	87	65	65	
7	Fee	55	64	45	
8	Grant	60	88	56	
9	Hasan	45	56	67	
10	MEAN	60.125			

To answer the following questions you will have to know how to highlight a rectangle A2 to E9 and sort by different rows.

1. What is the mean Maths score? _____

2. What is the mean English score?   _____

3. What is the mean Science score?   _____

4. What is the mean total score?   _____

5. What is Bhavna's total score?   _____

6. Who has the third highest Maths score?   _____

7. Who is in the top three scores for all subjects?   _____

8. How many pupils have above average Maths scores?   _____

9. Who has the fifth highest Science score?   _____

10. Who has the fourth highest total score?   _____

11. How many pupils have a higher English score than Fee?   _____

12. How many pupils have a higher Science score than Grant? _____

13. Who has the highest total score?   _____

14. Who has the lowest total score?   _____

© Bob Sykes
This page may be photocopied.

Remaindermind

Introductory activity

Pupils should have a good understanding of division and remainders and may need to be taught the meaning of the word 'divisor'.

Work through the following exercise with the pupils as an introductory activity.

I am thinking of a number between 11 and 30.
I divide this number by 3 and get a remainder of 1.
(On a sheet of paper write down 13, 16, 19, 22, 25, 28.)
I divide the same number by 5 and get a remainder of 2.
(Write down the numbers 12, 17, 22, 27.)
I divide the same number by 4 and get a remainder of 2.
(Write down the numbers 14, 18, 22, 26, 30.)
What is the number?
Answer: 22 – the only number in all three lists. Pupils may develop their own strategies and realize that only two guesses are needed in most cases.

Playing the game

This is a simple game which is best explained by example. Before each game starts, column A should be filled with the digit 1, from cell A2 through to cell A6. This will avoid ERRor messages appearing in column B. Pupils should be encouraged to discuss their strategies. They may wish to keep a running total of their score in some unused cells on the screen, eg

C2 | JON   C3 | 8

D2 | SUE   D3 | 5

Extension activities

• The range of choice for the mystery number may be extended to 11 to 50 and then finally 11 to 100, though different strategies may have to be involved (the range of divisors allowed should be extended to 9 in the latter case.)

Remaindermind

This is a game for two players

Player 1 enters a mystery number between 10 and 30 in cell A30.

Cell A30 is off the screen, so player 2 can't see it.

Player 2 has to guess this number. Player 2 types any number 2 to 6 in column A. The spreadsheet automatically divides the mystery number by the number in column A but only displays the remainder in column B.

Setting up the spreadsheet

A1 | Divisor   B1 | Remainder   B2 | =MOD(A30,A2)

B3 | =MOD(A30,A3)   B4 | =MOD(A30,A4)   B5 | =MOD(A30,A5)

B6 | =MOD(A30,A6)

Don't worry about ERRor messages at this point.

Imagine a game where player 1 puts the mystery number 17 in cell A30.

Player 2 enters 2 in cell A2. The remainder when 17 is divided by 2 is 1, so a 1 appears in cell B2. Player 2 enters 5 in cell A3. 2 appears in cell B3. Player 2 enters 6 in cell A4 and $17 \div 6$ is 2 remainder 5 so 5 appears in cell B4. Player 2 now has enough information to guess that the mystery number is 17. His score is 3, because he has had 3 guesses. The players swap over and take turns. The player with the lowest score is the winner.

Five guesses is the maximum allowed.

If player 2 guesses incorrectly, at any time, then he scores 6 points and his turn is over.

	A	B	C	D
1	Divisor	Remainder		
2	2	1		
3	5	2		
4	6	5		
5				
6				

To start a new game, clear all the guesses from A2 to A6, then put a new mystery number in A30.

Here is a number line to help you.

11   12   13   14   15   16   17   18   19   20   21   22   23   24   25   26   27   28   29   30

Throwing six dice

Introduction

The spreadsheet will show the scores when six dice are thrown. The activity is to find the most likely score.

The most likely score is 21, which has a probability of about 0.09.
The least likely scores are 6 and 36 which each would occur once in 46,656 attempts.
The reason for this is that only one combination of dice throws will give a total of 6, that is 1,1,1,1,1,1. There are many ways in which six separate scores on a dice can add up to 21, eg:

      6,6,6,1,1,1
      6,6,1,1,6,1
      5,5,5,4,1,1
      1,1,4,5,5,5   and so on.

Pupils can be asked to throw two dice and add the scores up. The most likely total score is 7 (probability 6/36) and the least likely scores are 2 and 12, each with a probability of 1/36.

Extension activities

• Pupils can draw bar charts of their results.

• Ask pupils to explain why not all totals are equally likely.

• Investigate the most likely total score if two dice are thrown, then three, four, and so on (two dice – 7; three dice – 11,12; four dice – 14; five dice – 17,18).

Throwing six dice

Setting up the spreadsheet

A1 | Die one   A2 | Die two   A3 | Die three   A4 | Die four

A5 | Die five   A6 | Die six   A7 | TOTAL

B1 | =INT(RAND()*6)+1   B7 | =B1+B2+B3+B4+B5+B6

Copy and fill cell B1 down to B6
Find which key you have to press to make the spreadsheet throw the dice another time and add the scores. (This might be the **calculate** or **recalculate** key, possibly the F9 function key.)

	A	B	C	D
1	Die one	3		
2	Die two	6		
3	Die three	5		
4	Die four	5		
5	Die five	1		
6	Die six	3		
7	TOTAL	23		
8				

Now try the following:

1. **Make a tally chart for all the totals between 6 and 36.**
    Press the calculate key 100 times and record your results.

    Which number is the most frequent total? _____

    Which number is the least likely total? _____

2. **Play a game for two people.**
    Player A chooses a target total between 6 and 36, player B chooses another. Players take it in turn to 'roll' the dice. The winner is the first to throw his **own** target total.

Starting points for further activities

Pupils' personal data

Collect data from pupils, eg name, gender, height, reach, birth month, eye colour, handspan. Set up a spreadsheet and enter the data. Use the graphing facilities on your spreadsheet to print pie-charts and graphs to display your data. Use the sorting facility to answer questions about rank orders. Compare the mean height of boys and girls. Are winter-born pupils taller?

Correlation

Use information on height and reach to produce scatter graphs.

League tables

Set up a spreadsheet to enter and update results from a football league. This can be updated throughout the duration of the league. Use the sort facility to re-order the league placings according to goals-scored, goals-conceded, away-wins, points, etc.

Timetable

Pupils can make a neat copy of their timetable using cell formatting to produce a professional finish. Ideas which can be incorporated (depending on the facilities of your spreadsheet) include use of different colours for different subjects, colour shading of cells, use of different font sizes, outline colours of cell borders, etc.

Similarly, pupils can produce a termly or yearly calendar. The teacher could produce the bare bones of a yearly school calendar and pupils could enter details.

Data cards

Some pupils may have an interest in playing cards that show various data about racing cars, footballers, space travel, dinosaurs, etc. Such cards lend themselves to treatment by spreadsheets which can reveal interesting facts and enable pupils to get a good understanding of how to handle data to advantage in order to make useful calculations of such things as rank order and averages. Use data from other sources too according to the interests of the pupils.

Personal uses

Pupils with computers at home might be encouraged to use spreadsheets for their own personal use as address books, financial records, personal diaries, etc.